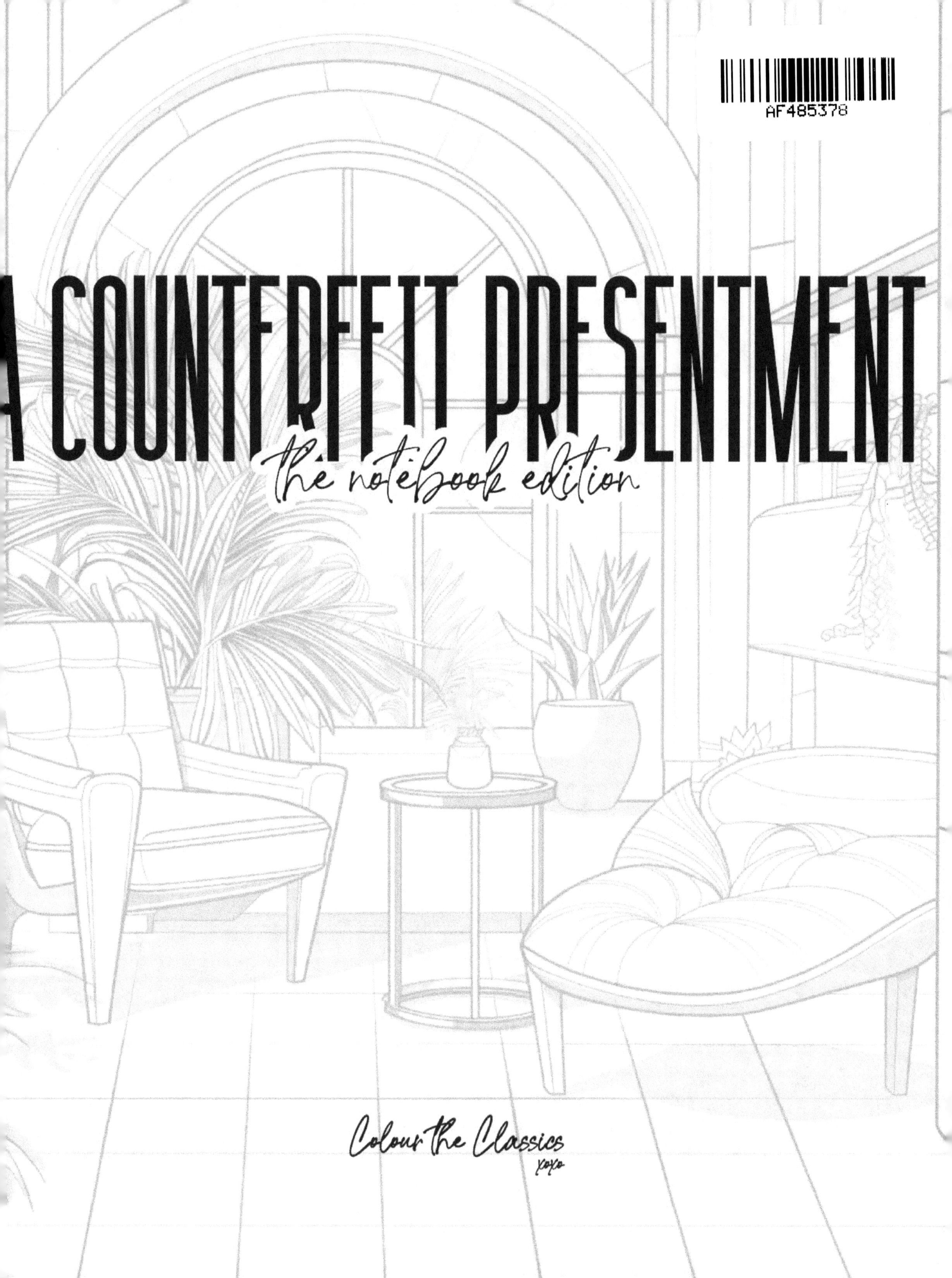

A COUNTERFEIT PRESENTMENT
the notebook edition
Colour the Classics
xoxo
AF485378

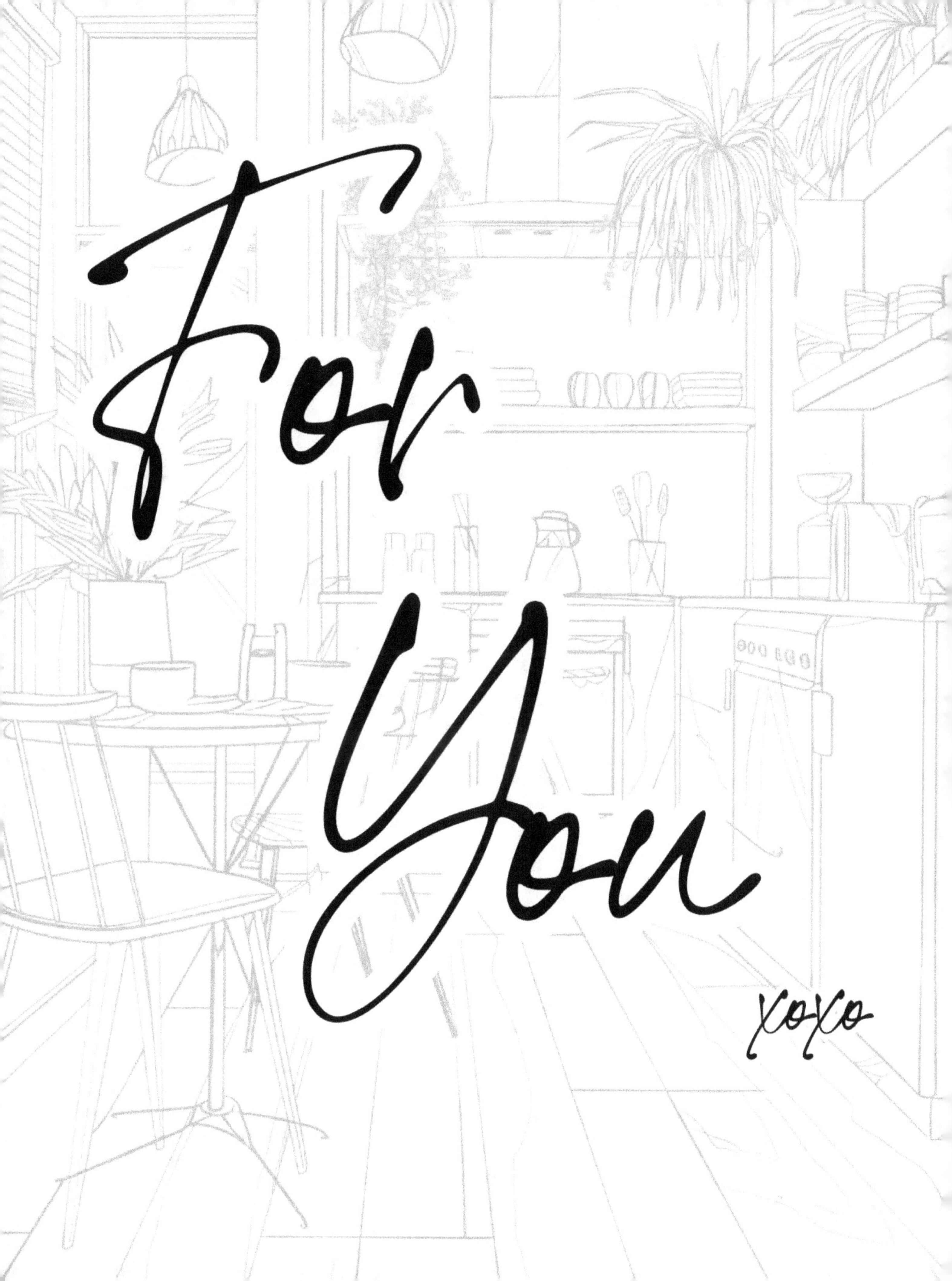

For
You
xoxo

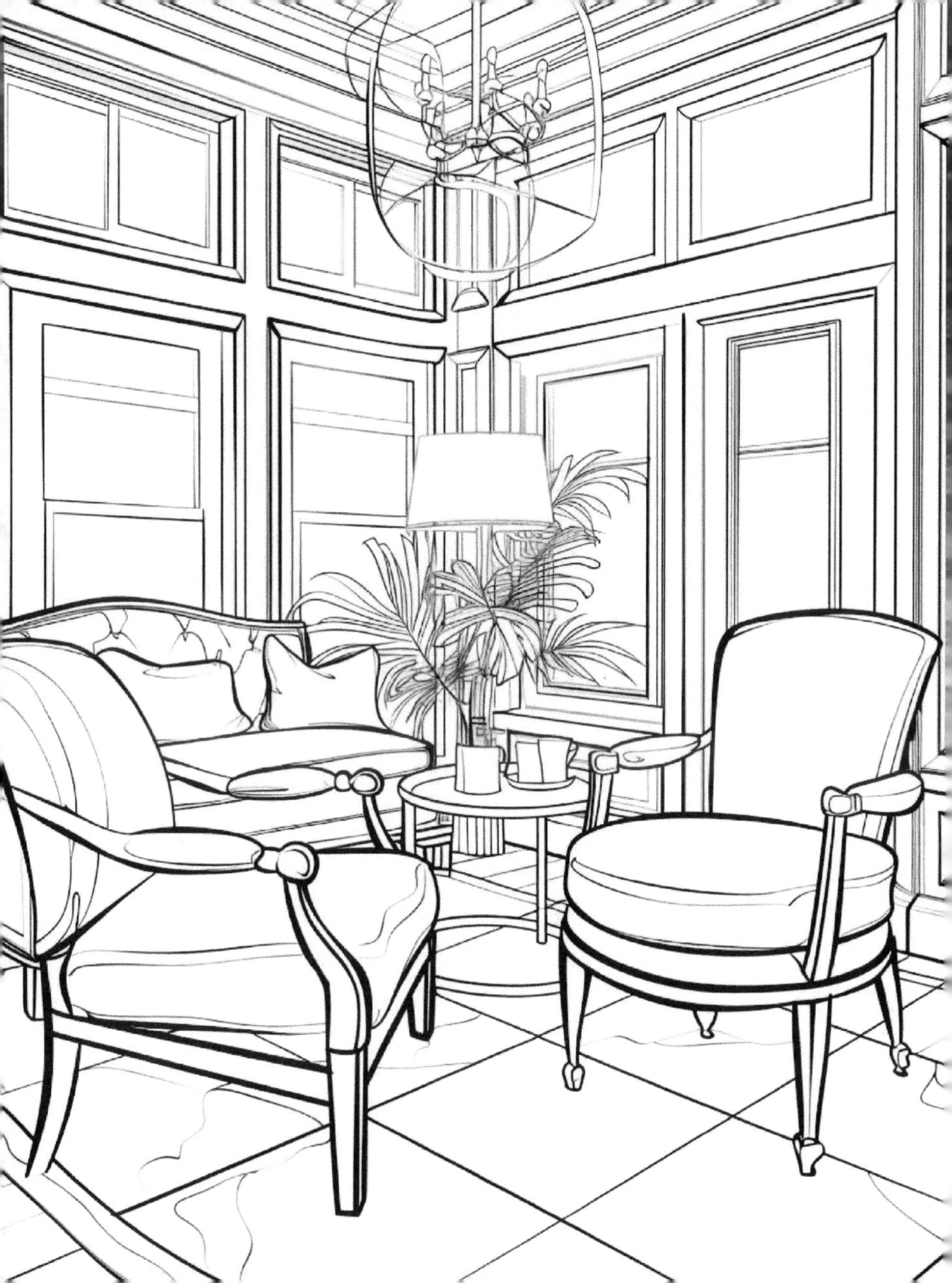

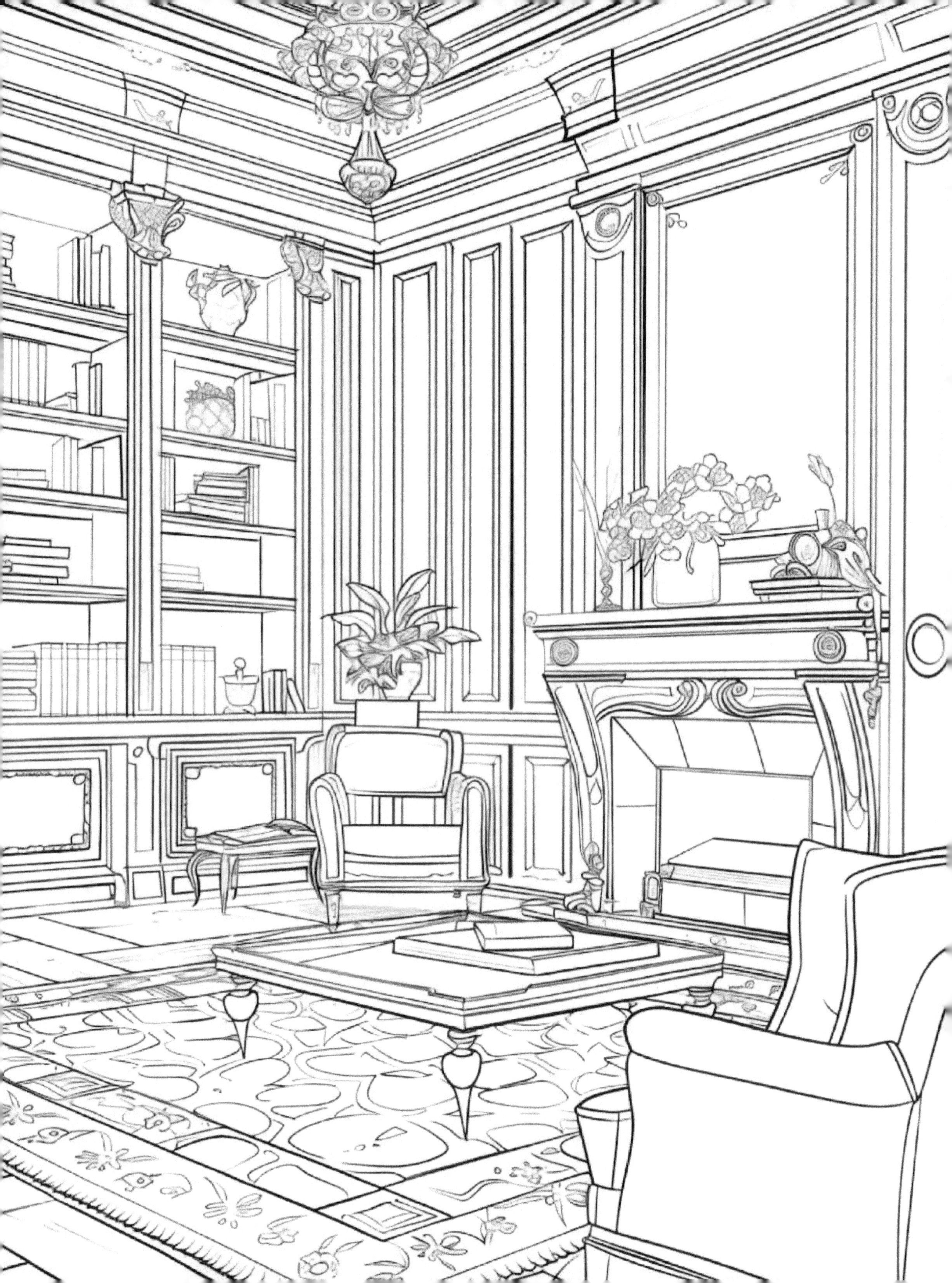

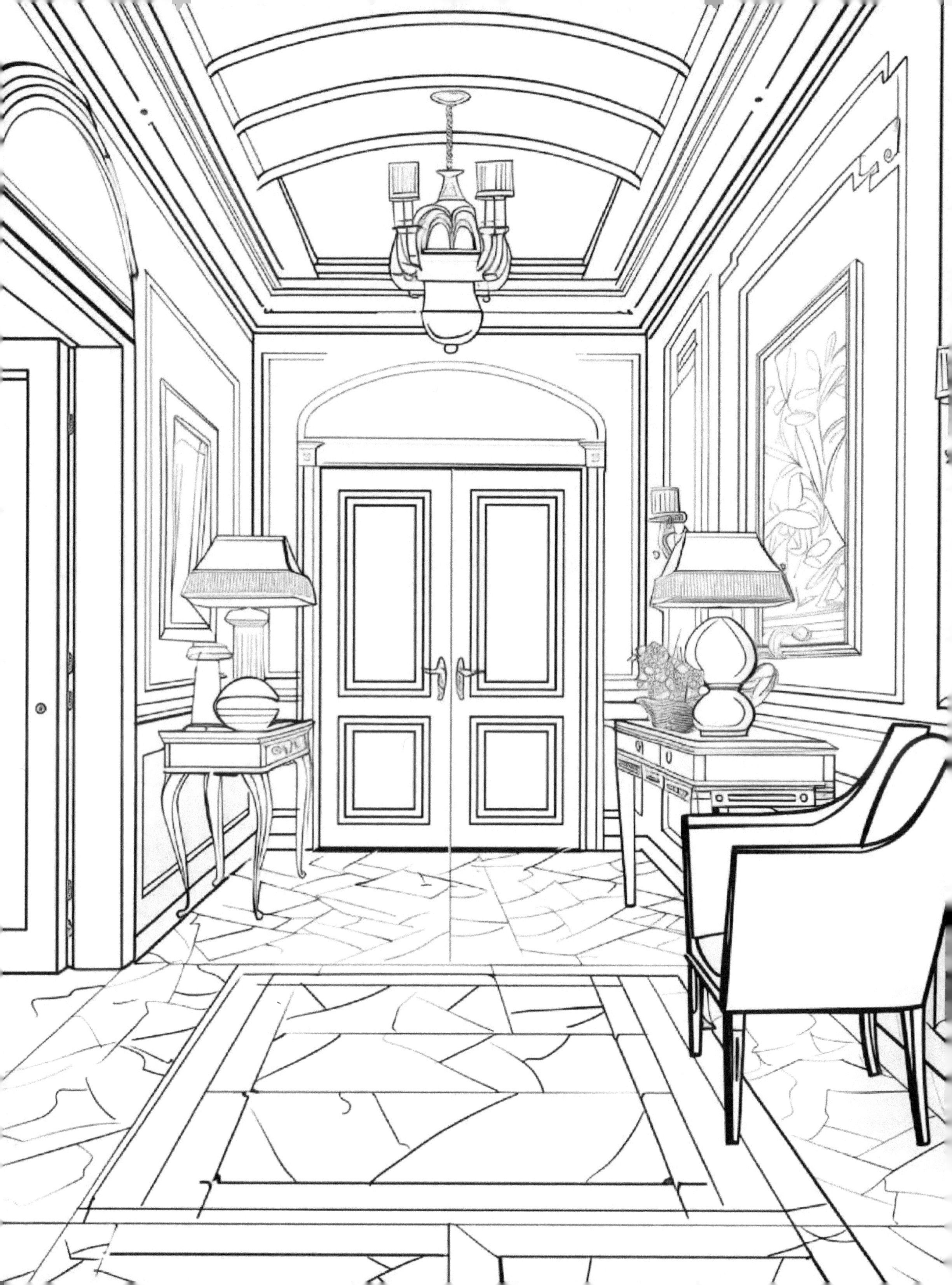

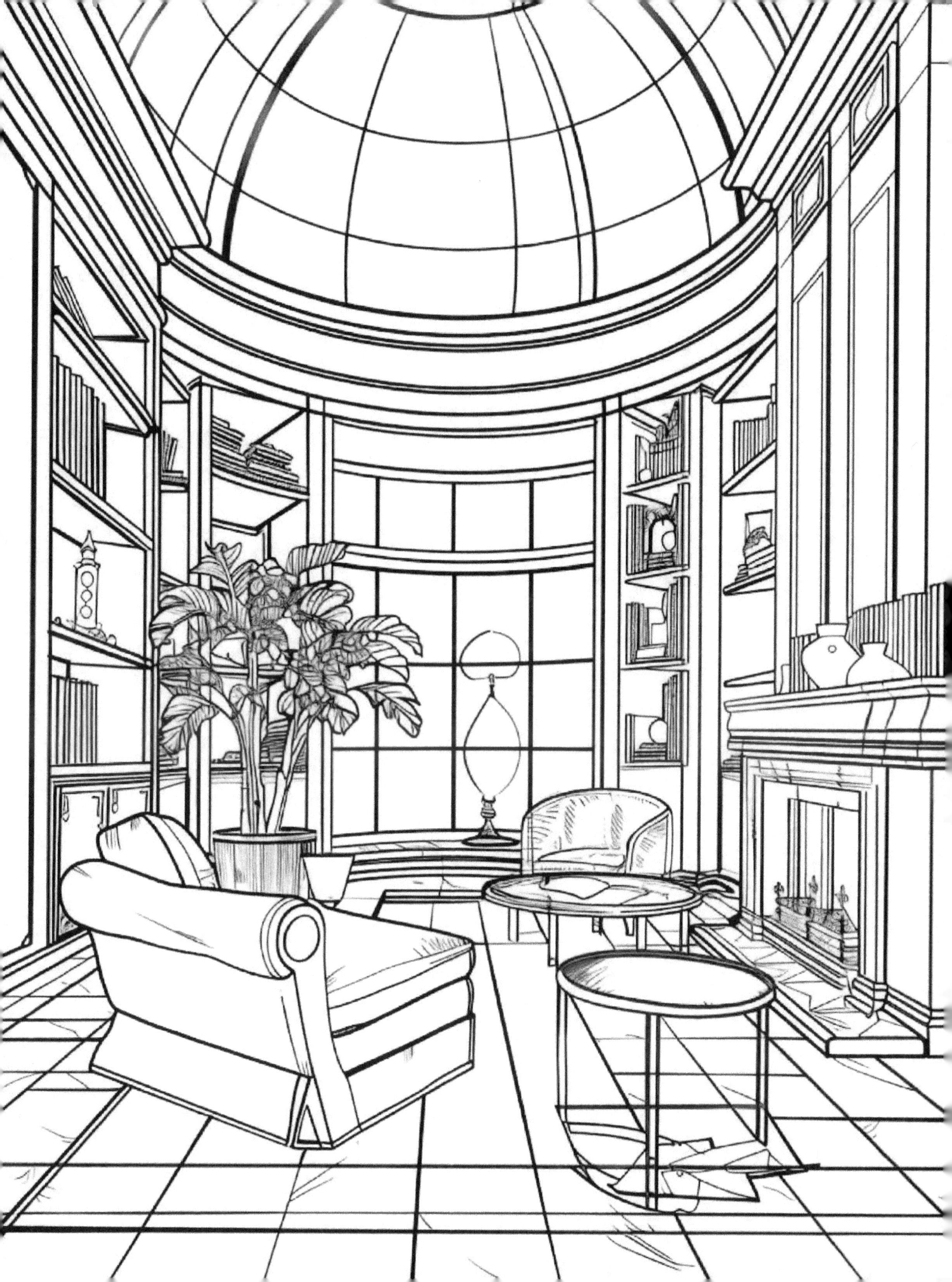

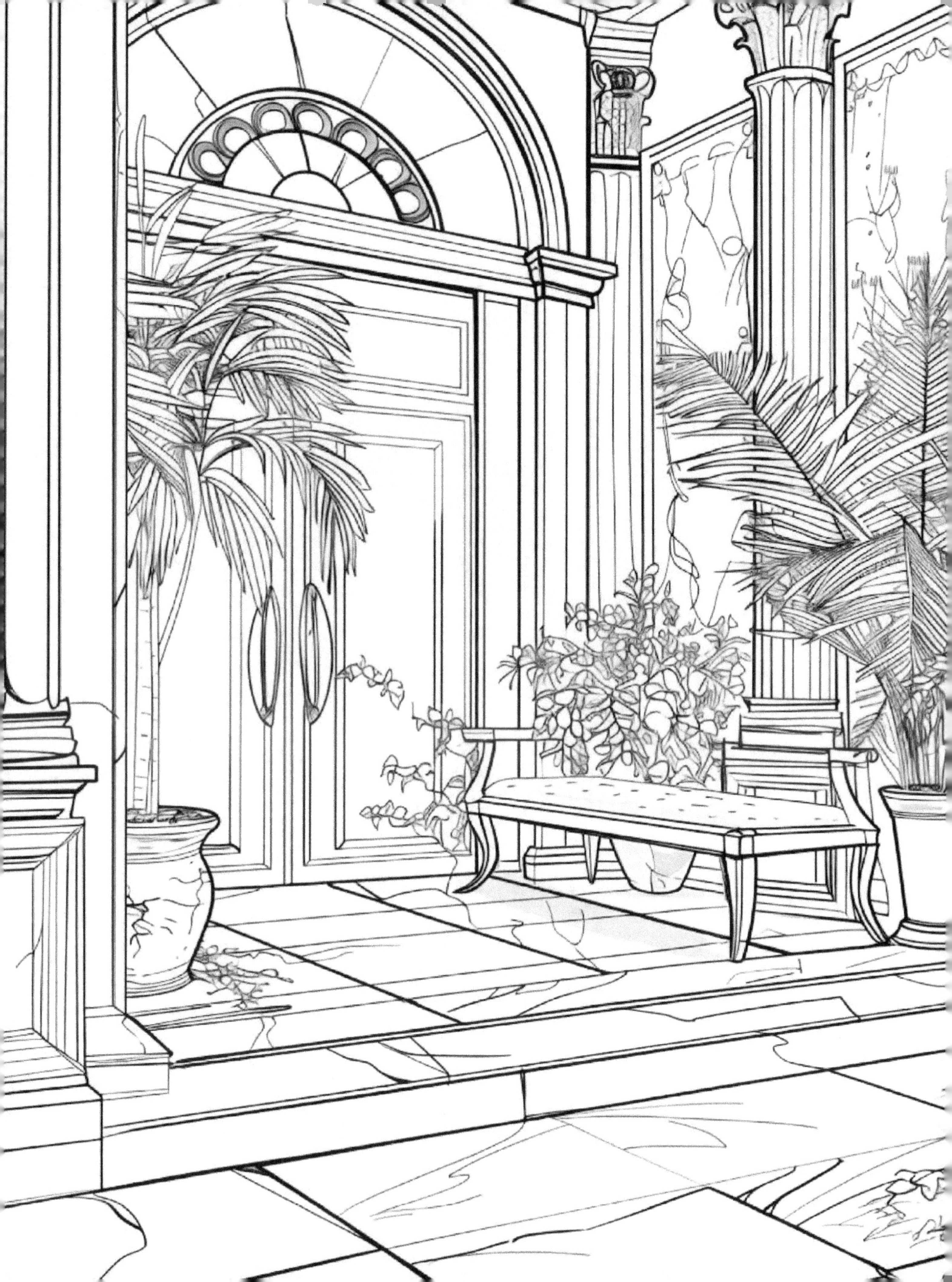

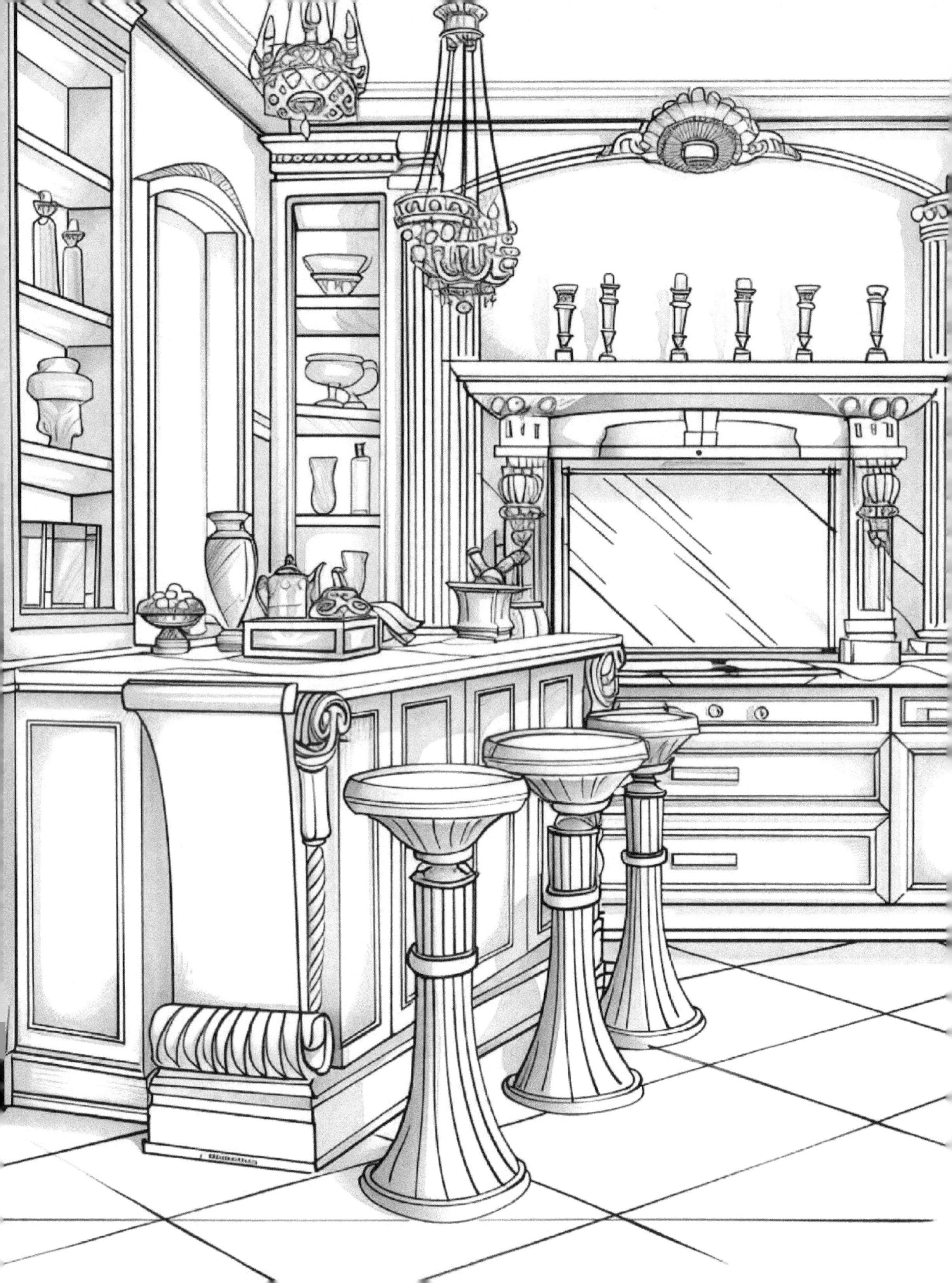

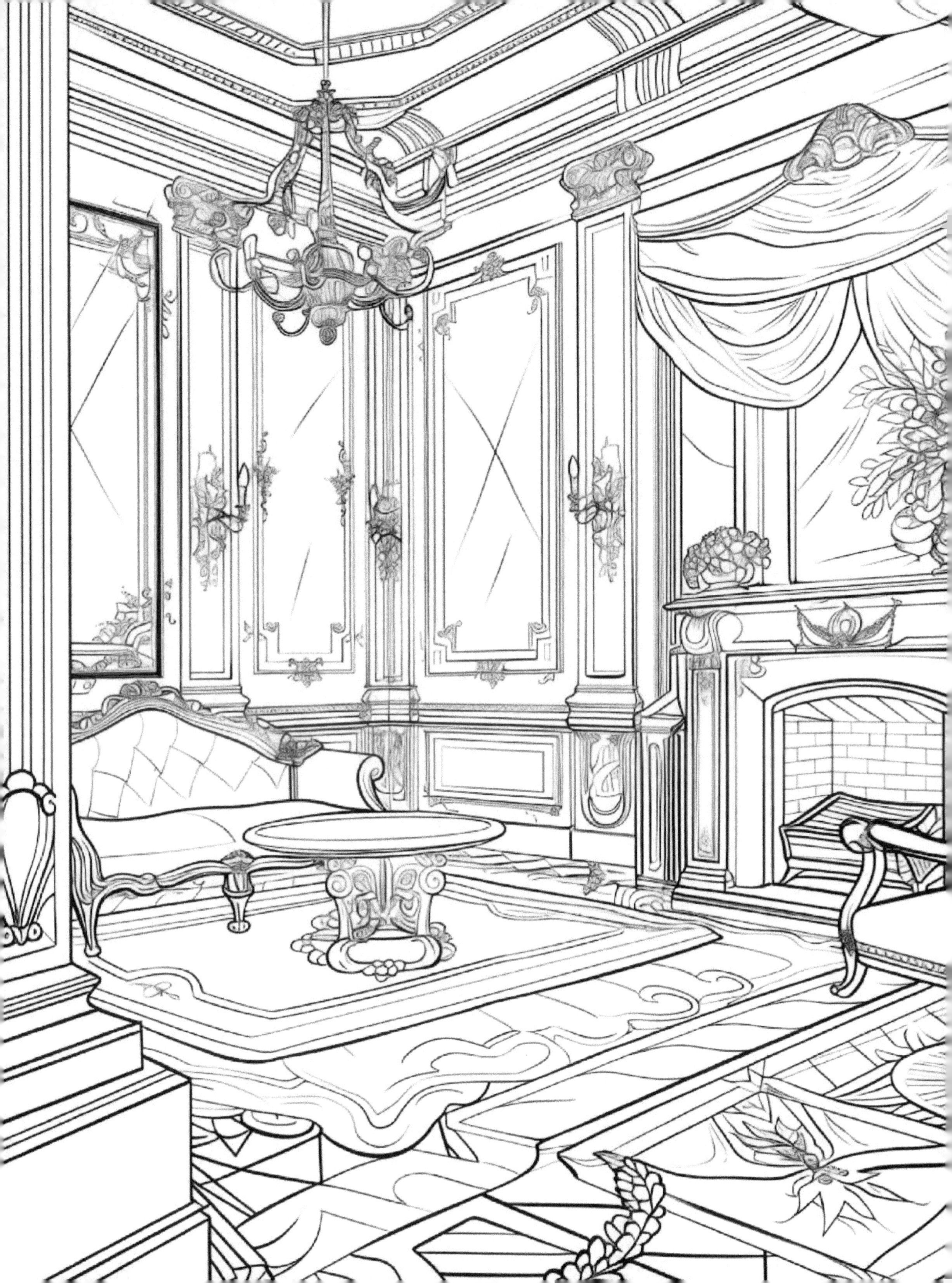

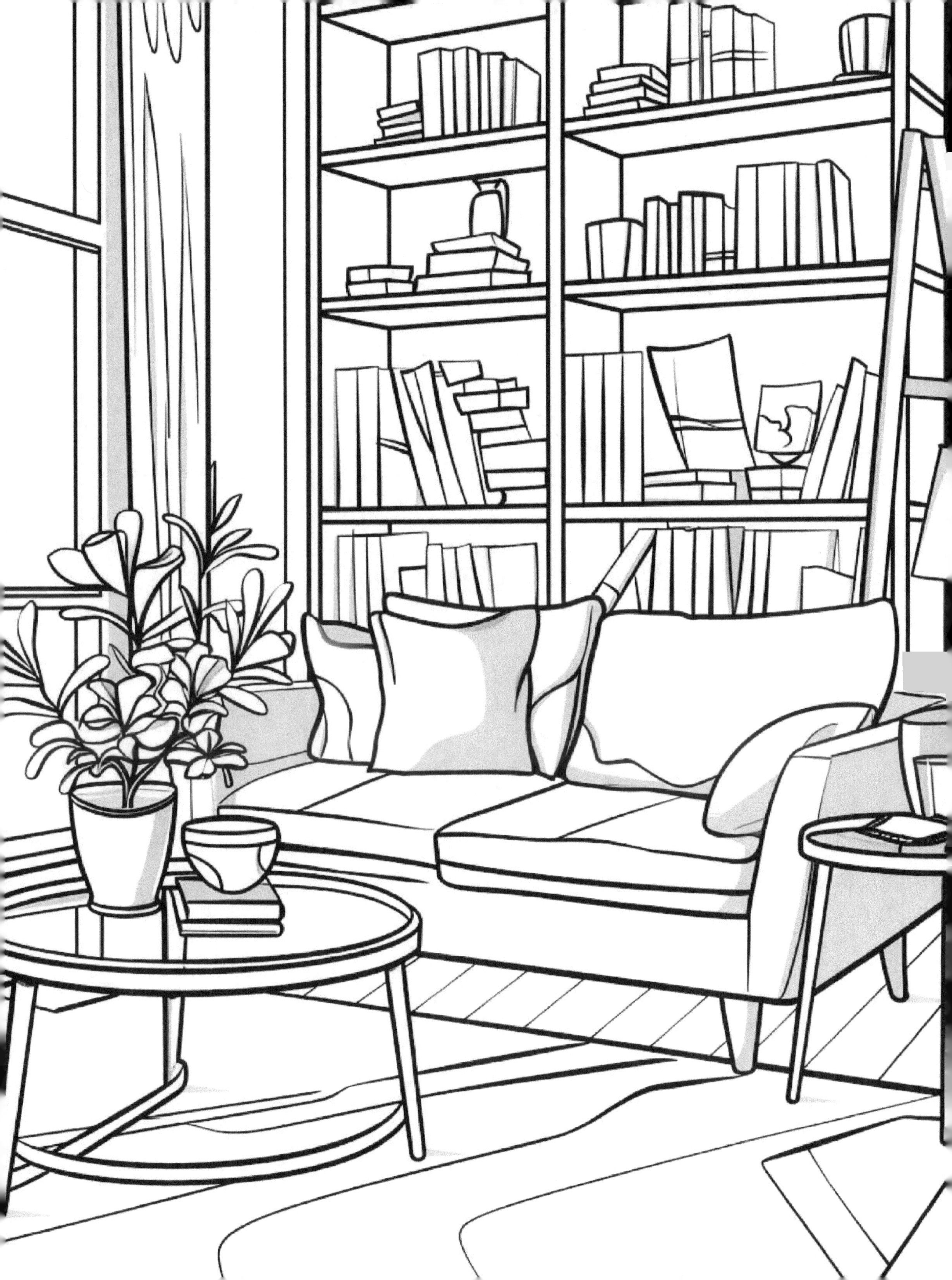

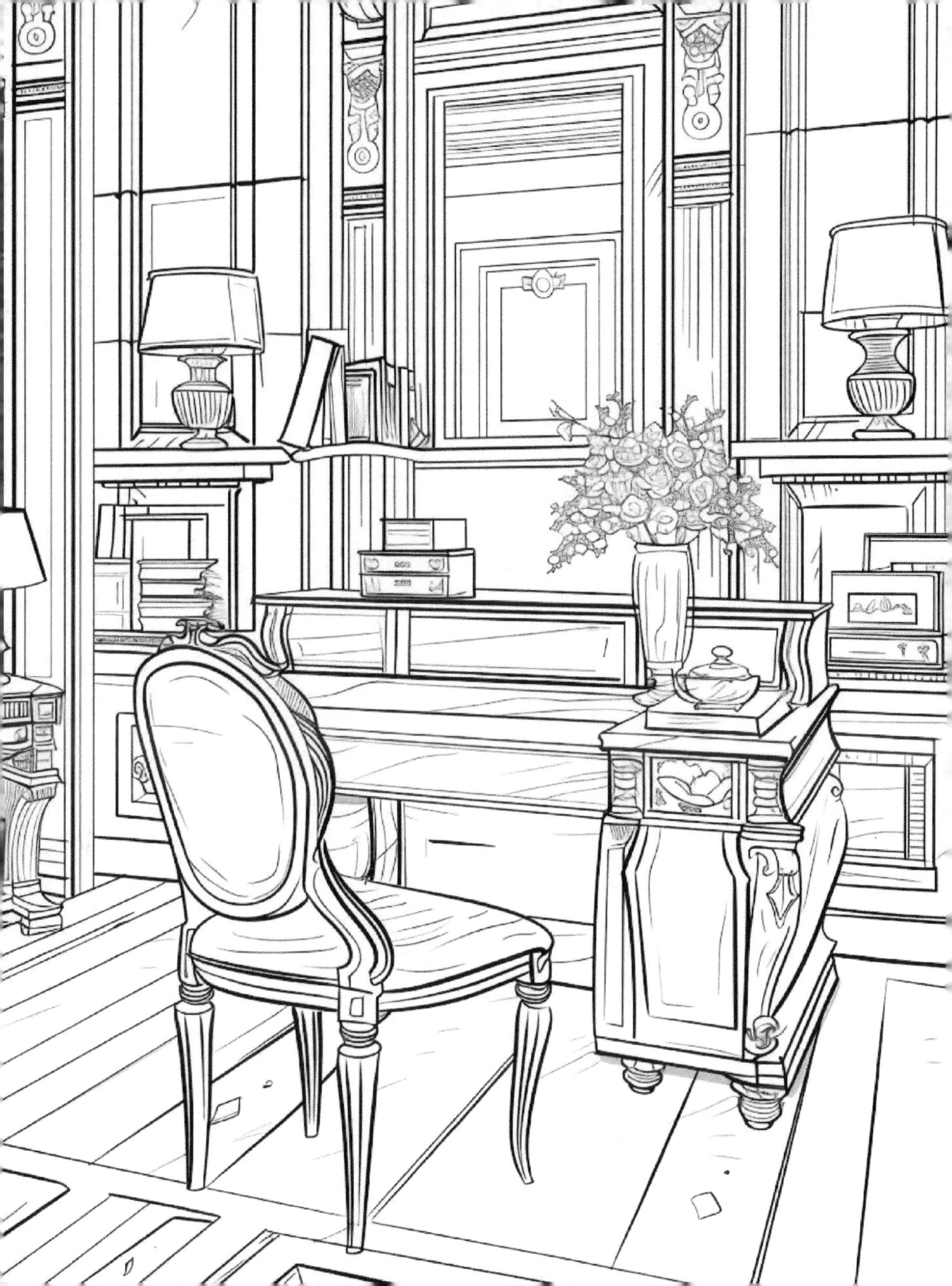

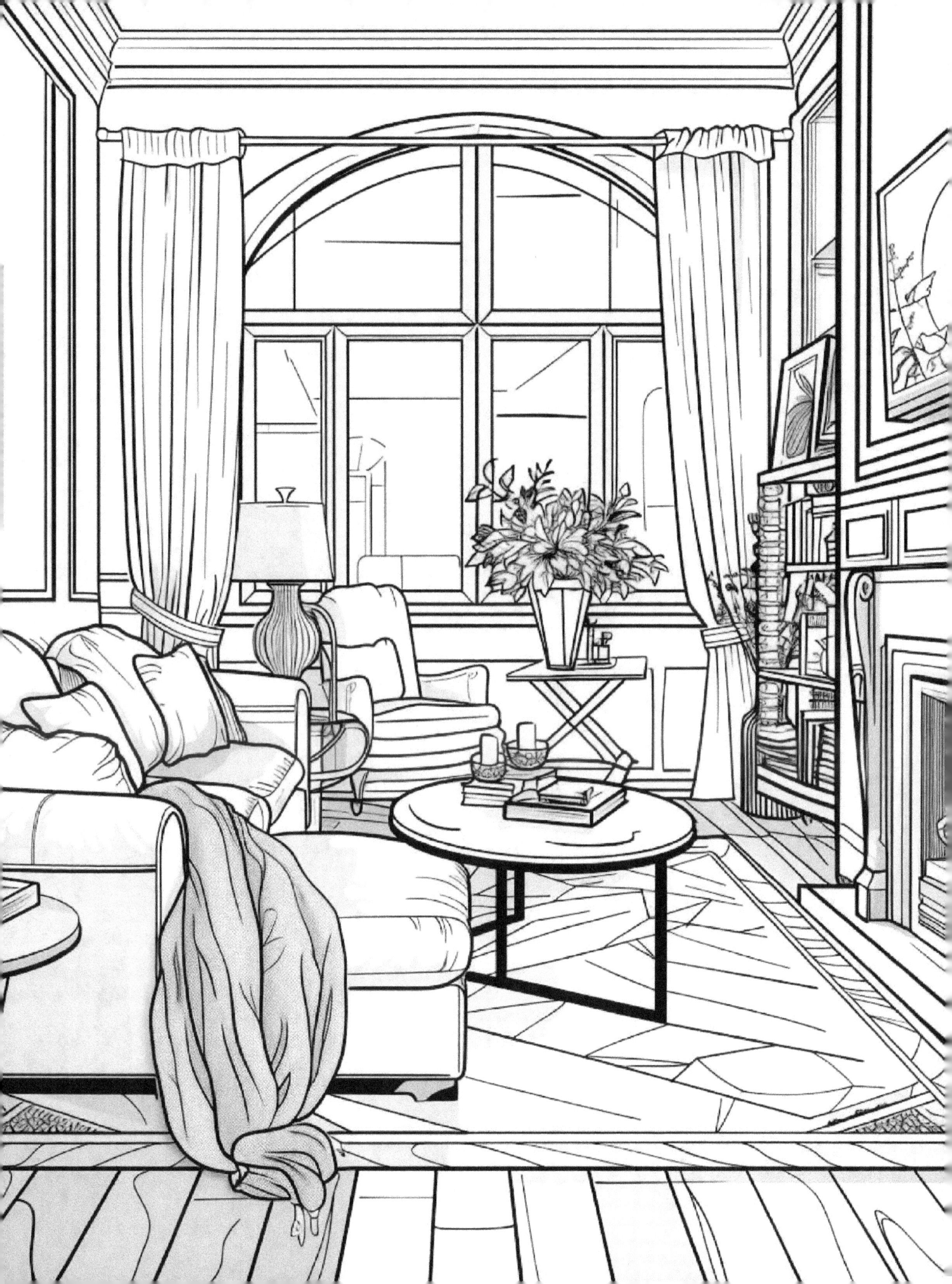

The

End